A

MYTHS

Robert Welch

Illustrated by Sara Walker

Appletree Press

for Elma and Denise

First published in 1996 by
The Appletree Press Ltd
19-21 Alfred Street
Belfast BT2 8DL

A catalogue record for this book is
available from the British Library.

ISBN 0 86281 501 0

9 8 7 6 5 4 3 2 1

Author's acknowledgements
My thanks to Mrs Lyn Doyle, who typed the manuscript, to
Joseph McLoughlin and Frank Reynolds, of the
Library of the University of Ulster, Coleraine, and
to Joseph McMinn, friend and colleague.

Contents

Introduction

☙

The tales translated here come from different periods of Irish literary tradition, but all of them draw upon the very oldest patterns of thought and feeling that influence the ways in which Irish people look at the world and respond to it. This is not to suggest that there is an exclusively Irish method of perception and that it is enshrined in these stories. I want, rather, to suggest that, as the clichés have it, "people are the same wherever you go", and yet, at the same time, "every beggar has his own way of walking." That is to say that if these stories are good stories - and I believe most readers will agree that they are outstanding pieces of narrative - then they will, at one and the same time, touch upon universal attitudes, persuasions, and outlooks, but also carry a distinctive coloration reflecting their Irish origin.

Fionnuala

or

The Children of Lir

❧

A long time ago, thousands of years ago, the Gaels invaded Ireland, and defeated the people who were there before them. These earlier people were known as the Tuatha Dé Danann, the people of the goddess Danu, she who gives her name to the Paps of Danu in Co. Kerry that you can see for miles around, even from the borders of Cork. The Tuatha Dé were sorely defeated by the Gaels at the Battle of Teltown, now in Co. Meath. After this the Tuatha Dé met together and in an attempt to strengthen their position they decided to elect one king who would rule over them all. The man they settled on in their conclave was Bodhbh Derg of Lough Derg on the Shannon in Connacht, on account of his own qualities and the respect they had for his father, the supreme deity of Newgrange, known as the Daghda.

Now this decision drove Lir, from the Fews in Co. Armagh,

into a rage because he wanted the kingship for himself. He left the meeting abruptly without asking leave or saying farewell or even speaking to anyone. Because of his insulting behaviour many of the Tuatha Dé wanted to follow him, kill him, and burn his house down but Bodhbh Dearg stopped them and said:

"No, don't do this. That man is too ardent a fighter not to make sure that no one will damage his property. And anyway, his disobedience and churlishness make me no less of a king."

They agreed to follow this advice, and Lir was left to his isolation and anger. So it went on for a long time. Then, suddenly, misfortune descended on Lir: his wife died after a three-day illness. This dismayed him and he became exhausted in spirit. When the story got to Bodhbh Dearg he took pity on the estranged and lonely man, and said:

"I could help Lir now, if he were to accept my friendship. Here at Lough Derg I have, as nurslings from Oilell of Aran, the three most attractive girls in Ireland - Aebh, Aoife, and Ailbhe. Lir can choose whichever of them he wishes on one simple condition, that he acknowledge me as head of the Tuatha Dé."

Messengers were sent north with this offer. Lir, overwhelmed by the kindness of the man he had insulted, accepted, and made haste to Lough Derg, arriving the following day with a retinue of fifty chariots. There, in front of Bodhbh Derg's palace, he made his submission and asked for forgiveness from his king. That night they feasted heartily before Lir was asked to choose between the three girls. They sat at the feast on the same seat as their foster-mother, Bodhbh Dearg's wife. Lir chose Aebh, because she was the eldest, and they slept together that night.

The festivities and celebration continued for a fortnight and then Lir took her back home with him up to Co. Armagh, where they had another wedding feast to mark their return.

Time went by and Lir and the young girl lived in joy and content. She bore him twins, Fionnuala and Aodh, and then she conceived again and gave birth to another set of twins, Fiachra and Conn. But misfortune struck once more and the young mother died giving birth the second time. This calamity would have driven the life out of Lir but for the comfort and solace he took from his four children.

Once again Lir's sad story came to the ears of Bodhbh Dearg and once again he took pity on him and offered him Aoife, Aebh's sister. Lir came south to take her; they slept in Bodhbh Dearg's palace; and then he took her back with him to the Fews. At first Aoife was delighted with her sister's children, and took pleasure in the joy they gave not only to Lir, but to anyone who met them. Bodhbh Dearg himself loved them and often came to visit the family, and would bring the children back to Lough Dearg to stay with him at his own palace. So dearly did their father love these four that he got them to sleep on couches in front of his own, and every morning he would wake up early to go and embrace them.

His devotion, however, awoke a fire of envy in Aoife, their stepmother. She started to hate them and resented the admiration they won from everyone. To draw attention to herself she pretended to be sick for a whole year, but even though great care and concern was shown towards her she still wasn't satisfied. She decided to get rid of them.

One day she had her chariot prepared for her and told the children to climb into it and go along with her. Fionnuala knew in her own mind that her stepmother had planned something evil against them but she could not refuse what seemed an ordinary command even though she could feel the malice in Aoife. When she got the children some way from Lir's house she pulled a sword from its scabbard in the chariot intending to kill them

but a womanly instinct combined with fear of physical violence stopped her. In fury and panic she drove the chariot on to Lough Derravaragh in Co. Westmeath. She loosed the horses on the strand and told the children to climb down from the chariot, to take off their clothes, and to wash themselves in the lake, saying that they were covered in dirt from the long drive.

Once again Fionnuala knew that evil was afoot, but she found it impossible to disobey a sensible request. They all did as they were told, and entered the cold water of the lake. When they were swimming around, Aoife, who was trained in the arts of magic, struck the water's surface with an enchanted rod, and immediately the four lovely bodies before her changed their shapes into four swans as white as snow. Their bodies changed as they were swimming and when the transformation was complete the four shapes all turned in unison, as swans do, and then Fionnuala spoke strangely through her new throat:

"What you have done to us is evil. It is an evil return for all the friendship and care that has been shown to you. Though your magic is strong it's not as strong as the power our father and his friends will bring against you in vengeance. This act of yours will finish you. But please, even if only to lessen the harshness of the punishment that awaits you, put some limit on this enchantment. Give it some end."

"Alright, I'll do that", Aoife replied. "But you're going to regret having asked this favour. You'll stay as you are until a woman of the south lies with a man of the north. And, on top of that, you'll continue in these shapes until you've spent three hundred years on this lake, three hundred on the Sea of Moyle between Ireland and Scotland, and three hundred in the Atlantic

off Erris in Mayo. Those will be your adventures and this is your fate from now on."

The swans looked at her and bent their heads in sorrow. Their grief awoke some pity in Aoife and she said:

"There's nothing to be done now to mitigate this curse. You will continue to be able to speak. Also you will sing music that will be like no other music and it will ravish listeners with sweetness. You will continue to be able to think and even though your lives will be harsh you will never completely despair in spite of your pitiful condition."

She left them there and when she had gone they swam out

into the deep reaches of the lake, paddling slowly.

Aoife went on from Lough Derravaragh to Lough Derg to her foster-father's palace. After Bodhbh Dearg had welcomed her he asked her why she had come alone without the children.

"Lir has started to dislike you and believes you have always hated him. He wouldn't trust you with his children anymore, he says."

"I don't believe you", said Bodhbh Dearg. "I love his children more than I do my own and Lir knows that."

He left the woman in her chamber. Having become sure that she had done something wrong he sent messengers north to the Fews. When they came there Lir asked them what had brought them.

"We've come", one said, "because of your children."

"What has become of them?" asked Lir.

"Are they not here with you?"

"No", replied Lir. "They went with Aoife in her chariot to Bodhbh Dearg's house. What has happened to them?"

"Aoife said you would not trust Bodhbh Deag with them."

"There is malice at work", said Lir. He knew now that Aoife had destroyed or ruined them in some way. He found out that she had gone to Lough Derravaragh on her way to Bodhbh Dearg and he set off next morning. When the children saw his retinue they swam to shore and uttered a song of welcome. Lir came down to the water's edge to these strange creatures who could speak and sing and asked them why they had human voices.

"We", said Fionnuala, "are your four children bewitched by our stepmother out of envy."

"Can this spell be reversed?" asked Lir, heartstruck.

"No", Fionnuala said, and told him the term of their enchantment and the conditions.

When they heard this Lir's people gave three roars of sorrow.

"Can you come ashore? Can you be with us even in your swan form and keep us company? I don't know how I can live without your presence in my house."

"We can't be with human people anymore", said Fionnuala. "We are birds. But we can speak and sing of our sorrow and that will soothe any troubled person. Stay near here tonight and our song will comfort you and lighten your sadness, my father."

So they stayed and listened to the magical music and slept sweetly in spite of their grief.

The following day he went to Bodhbh Dearg. When he was inside the palace Bodhbh Dearg asked him whey he had not brought the children. Lir replied:

"You have been lied to and I most grievously wronged by Aoife over there, your own nursling. She has, through her magic, changed them into four swans."

A violent spasm of shock ran through Bodhbh Dearg's body, and he said to her:

"The children will, in time, be released from this spell of yours, but you will never be freed from what I am going to do to you. What do you loathe and fear most of all?"

She had to reply. Her guilt and his force made her.

"The demons of the air."

"That is what you are this moment", and he struck her with his druid rod and in a dark flurry she was gone into the volumes of the air, where she flies to this day.

Then Bodhbh Dearg went to Lough Derravaragh, where he encamped and listened to the swan-music, which calmed his sorrow. From that time on the Tuatha Dé Danann would come to the strand to listen to their singing, and the Gaels too as the years went past, because no one had ever heard such delightful harmonies of sound to enchant the ear and fill the mind with pleasure. Not only did their singing allay the distress of even the most unhappy man or woman, the swans also recited stories and poems and held conversations with learned men and their students. So they continued for three hundred years until one night Fionnuala said to the others:

"Do you know this is our last night here?"

They did not, and the three boys were saddened because being in contact with the Tuatha Dé and even the Gaels was closer to being human than to be out on the fierce waters of the Sea of Moyle. In the morning they swam to the strand where Lir and Bodhbh Dearg were standing and they sang a poem of farewell before taking off together into the bitter sky northwards to Moyle. They were sorely missed by everyone, and it was decreed from that day forward that no-one in Ireland should ever kill a swan, on pain of death or the most severe penalty.

When the four birds saw the bare cliffs and cold sea of Moyle they were filled with dismay. They settled into the freezing water, and their webs and wings grew numb with the shock. It took them a long time to grow used to the cold.

After a few months had passed there came a storm of thunder, snow, and terrible winds. Fionnuala said to her brothers, between the peals of thunder and the shrieking gusts, that they would probably be separated in the tempest, and that they should decide on one place where they would meet again:"Let us meet at Seal Rock, as we all know where that is", she said.

Throughout the night the wind howled, the waves boiled in a white seething foam, driving every way; the lightning flashed, its brilliant light only showing the heaving masses of water. The four were scattered miles apart. As morning broke a slow calm settled on the sea and Fionnuala, alone on the stilling waters, sang a lament for her lost brothers. All through that day and the following night she stayed at Seal Rock. On the second morning she saw Conn toiling towards her, his head hanging down, his plumage all bedraggled. Her heart leapt when she saw him coming towards her in the morning light. Then, next, Fiachra arrived, so cold and tired he could not speak a word to her or to Conn. Fionnuala spread her wings to cover them both and warm them.

"If Aodh were now here all would be well", she said.

And then, almost immediately, they saw him. But, strangely, his head was dry, and white, and neat; and his feathers smooth and lovely. Without asking him how he had escaped the terrors of the storm, she drew him to her breast, and they stayed still for hours, on the calm sea, their hearts beating. Aodh later told them that a massive wave had swept him high up on to a sandy beach, leaving him on top of a deep pile of soft seaweed, where he'd stayed and watched the storm wear itself out.

"That was a terrible night", she said, "and there will, I am sorry to say, be many more like it until our time here is at an end."

And indeed there were many nights like this, but there came one night which surpassed all others for bitter cold, with frost, wind, and thick snow. The sea-water around the black basalt coast froze solid, and their feet and wings stuck to the rocks, so that they were imprisoned in a field of ice. As they pushed with

their thighs and wings in vain attempts to get free they worked their feathers and skin off their limbs, exposing their bloody flesh to the salt ice. Fionnuala thought they would all die, either from the cold, or from the salt that ate into their open wounds. But eventually the ocean thawed, and though it took a long time, their deep sores healed up.

One day they swam westwards from Moyle to the mouth of the river Bann. When they arrived there, they rode on the huge surge of water pouring out into the sea. They saw a great troop

of riders, brilliantly attired, riding along the estuary-side, coming from the south-west.

"Do you know these riders?" Fionnuala asked her brothers.

They said they didn't, and then she swam ahead towards the sandy shoreline, her brothers following. When the riders saw the four swans at the shore, they rode down to them. They were so many that they filled the sandy beach of the estuary. The two leaders of the troop were Aodh and Fergus, the sons of Bodhbh Dearg, and with them a third of the host of the Tuatha Dé Danann, charged with finding the children of Lir. They had been searching for them on the bleak and wild coastline of the Moyle many times over the years, but had not found them. Fionnuala asked how her father was and how things were faring for the Tuatha Dé. Bodhbh Dearg's sons told her that they continued to visit each other, feasting at Lir's palace and at their father's on the Shannon, content but for the absence of the four lovely children. They never failed to remember the happy times when they were small and in their own shapes, sleeping in their father's arms, or even when they consoled the sore at heart at Lough Derravaragh.

Aodh and Fergus, after conversing with the children, turned the massive host back towards the Fews and told Lir they had met them at the mouth of the Bann. This made him happy, to think they were still alive, but even though the Tuatha Dé sent many other search parties to the Moyle coastline they were never found again.

When their second appointed term of three hundred years was past they took to the air one day, with grateful hearts to be leaving such a place, and flew westwards and south out to Erris off the Mayo coast, where they were to spend their last three centuries. Although the Atlantic sea was milder most of the time, the seas were vaster and often more turbulent even than those at Moyle. Although it happened less frequently there could, still, be devasting cold off Erris.

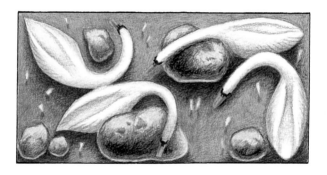

One night the Atlantic froze over from Achill up to Erris and the children were stuck fast in ice again. Because they thought, after leaving Moyle, that they would not ever again have to suffer such extremity of pain, the brothers would not be consoled, despite Fionnuala's attempts to raise their spirits.

They suffered the long Atlantic winters, with their continuous downpours, fog, and doleful days of grey light. But there were summers, too, amongst the many islands, and the scent of myrtle wafting off the bogland slopes above them. At length their time was up and Fionnuala told her brothers that they all could go back to Lir's fort in the Fews. Gladly they flew from the Atlantic across the country, over the long lake of Lough Erne. When they got to the mound where Lir's palace had been all they found was a bare green hillock overgrown with clumps of nettles. They circled over the place where there used to be a throng of talking people, shouting, the clank of armour being shaped, the loud snorts of horses, the smells of the bakehouse and the kitchen. Now there was silence and the sad movements of the grey nettles in the wind. They settled on a patch of green where the hearth used to be and sang their mournful song. Early next day, they spread their wings and flew across Ireland back to Erris, where they found a small lake on the island of Inishglora. From there they flew off each day, feeding off the plentiful fish that teemed in the waters between Achill and Erris. So they continued for a while.

It was during this period that St Patrick came back to Ireland, bringing with him the Gospel of Our Lord Jesus Christ, baptizing the Irish people, founding churches throughout the land, and winning many followers who equalled him in devotion and piety. One of these was a man called St Mochaemóg, who was called to the life of a hermit. He went into the lonely parts of Mayo, and then eventually found Inishglora where he decided to build a small stone church by the little lake with four swans swimming on it.

The first night he spent by the lakeside the brothers were frightened by the faint tolling of his little bell, which he rang during his evening prayers. But Fionnuala knew Mochaemóg meant them no harm and she urged them to sing with him as he began to intone the psalms over the water. When he heard the lovely sounds coming out of the darkness he was amazed, and prayed that it be revealed to him where that music came from and who made it. In the night an angel came to him and told him their sad tale. The next day he went to the lakeside and asked them if they were the children of Lir.

"We are", said Fionnuala.

"Thanks be to God and his blessed mother", said the saint. "I've been sent to this island to redeem you. Please come ashore and be with me."

So they did, and when the saint had built his tiny church, they would hear Mass and sing the psalms along with him. Fearing they might fly away from him and revert to the wild, he had a smith make two silver chains, one to bind Fionnuala and Aodh, the other for Conn and Fiachra. They were happy to be chained in this way because it gave them great pleasure to be with the holy man. The reputation of the swans spread all over

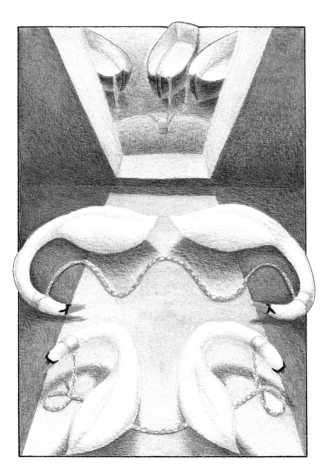

Connacht, and visitors began to come on pilgrimage, to see these ancient birds and hear them sing.

Now the king of Connacht at this time was Lairgréan and his wife was Deoch, daughter of the king of Munster, so a man of the north had married a woman from the south, fulfilling the last condition of the breaking of the enchantment. However, when Deoch visited the island, she wanted the swans for her own house and asked her husband to command the saint to give them up to the royal palace. But he would not agree to this, and she, angry that he would not indulge her, swore she'd not sleep with him again until she had the swans about her, and stormed out of the house travelling back south to her father. Lairgréan sent men after her, to tell her he had relented, and they caught up with her at Killaloe and brought her back. However when he sent his messengers to the saint Mochaemóg refused to hand the swans over. The king went himself to Inishglora, strode into the church and seized the swans by their chains from the altar, where they were sitting. Roughly hauling them out of the church, he headed back towards the boat by the shore. Handling them in this brutal manner, he chafed the swansdown off their necks and heads, and the three brothers turned into three bony old men, and Fionnuala into a bloodless hag. When he saw what he had done Lairgréan was ashamed and horrified. The saint was furious with rage and dismay. Fionnuala said, in a feeble ancient voice:

"Please, the two of you, do not quarrel. Mochaemóg, please baptize us. We will die very soon. And when we die place Fiachra and Conn on each side of me, and put Aodh into my arms."

The saint baptized the four ancient creatures, and they passed away there and then, their souls flying straight to heaven where Jesus welcomed them after their long suffering. They were buried on Inishglora as Fionnuala had requested, and an ogham stone was raised over the grave with their names inscribed on it.

The saint pronounced a curse on the king and his covetous wife and they too died not long after.

[This retelling is based upon the text edited and compiled by Seán Ua Ceallaigh in *Tri Tuagha na Scéaluidheachta* (1927).]

Macha

or
The Pangs of Ulster

❦

The name Emhain Macha, Navan Fort in Co. Armagh, means the "Twins of Macha" and the terrible story of how these twins were born explains how, in ancient times, whenever Ulster was in danger, its menfolk suffered the pangs of childbirth. The story begins in a remote part of Ulster, in the heart of Pictish territory, somewhere north of where Ballymena is now, and south of Ballymoney. Crunnchu was a wealthy farmer living out in the wilds in solitude and isolation. In spite of this he prospered, and his wife bore him many sons who helped him on his farm. However, while some of the boys were still very young he was widowed, but he did not remarry, and he lived alone.

One day, while lying on his couch taking a rest after eating, a beautiful young woman came to him, exquisitely dressed in the finest silk, swift and elegant in her movements. She did not speak to him, but immediately bent down to the hearth and started to kindle a fire. All day she walked around the house, not saying a word, and in the evening she found a bowl for kneading dough, and a sieve for flour and she made bread. She prepared meat too for the household and fed the men. At nightfall she took up the milk pails and went out to the cow byre. Coming back into the house with the pails full she turned to the right inside the threshold to bring good luck to the family and the house, then went to sit in a chair beside Crunnchu. When the men and boys went to bed she stayed behind at first, banking down the fire; then, turning again to the right she went to Crunnchu's bed and awakened him with her light touch.

So she continued, living with him, and caring for him until she became pregnant.

At this time the men of Ulster used to hold a great assembly or fair, known as an "aonach", when all of them would gather together to celebrate their unity, and one-ness, the word "aonach" coming from "aon", meaning one. Now while his wife was pregnant Crunnchu decided to go to this fair like everyone else.

"No, do not", said his woman, whose name, he had discovered, was Macha. "Do not go," she said, "because if you do you will tell everyone who I am and that will be the end of us."

"I promise", he said, "that I will not mention you or refer to you in any way."

And so, he went along. The field was full of people, with their horses and chariots, and banners flying over the crowd. Everyone was dressed in their brightest clothes - blue, orange, red, and green. There were competitions and games of all kinds: horse-racing, throwing the dice, spear-casting, parades, displays, cavalcades. In the middle of the afternoon, which was the high

point of the fair, the king's chariot and horses were brought before the crowd. The king challenged any riders to race against his team but his equipage beat all comers. The bards and poets recited their praise poems to the king, gravely intoning their descriptions of his valour and prowess, and extolling the achievements of his team of horses. Crunnchu was listening to all of this and he grew restless, knowing that his wife was better than anyone or anything in the field that day. Eventually, he could restrain himself no longer and blurted out:

"My wife, Macha, can run faster than the king's horses."

"Seize him and throw him into the dungeon", he said "and fetch his woman to see if she is as good as he says."

Everyone laughed. But the king remained grim and determined. Messengers were sent. When they got to Crunnchu's isolated farm, Macha knew that trouble lay ahead.

"We've come", a messenger said, "to give you the opportunity of releasing your husband, who has been locked up for boasting that you were faster on your feet than the king's team of racing horses."

"This is terrible", she said. "I am pregnant and going into labour even now. That was a stupid thing for him to say."

"True", said the messenger, "but he will die unless you race."

"What will be will be", she said.

When she got to the fair, they all stared.

"It is wrong for you all to be looking at a woman in my condition. I should not be here. I cannot race in the throes of my birth-pangs."

"Well", said the king turning to a group of laughing men behind him, "who will go to give the farmer a good hacking? You either race or he dies."

"Just wait, even for a little while, until I bring forth what is inside me," said Macha.

"No, now, you race this moment", said the king.

"You and your kind will regret this forever", she said. "Your shame will last for nine generations. Alright, bring the horses and set them here beside me."

And so it was done. The horses were brought up and the race begun. She ran so fast that by the time she reached the end of the course she had cleared enough space to allow her to cross over in front of the galloping horses. Then she collapsed and screamed out in pain as she writhed on the ground. A girl and a boy were born there in the field, and these were the two that gave Emhain Macha its name, the Twins of Macha. As the woman howled in agony all energy left the men standing looking on, in silence and shame. She spoke:

"What you have done is your own disgrace. When things go hard for Ulster you will all be as weak as a woman when her time has come. And you will continue that way for as long as a woman spends in labour: five days and four nights. And this curse will last for nine generations."

And so it was. So that when Medhbh of Connacht attacked Ulster seeking to carry off the bull of Cooley, all the men were laid low by this debility; all that is except Cú Chulainn, the defender of the north, for he was British, and therefore not one of the men of Ulster.

[This retelling is based on *Noínden Ulad*, preserved in *The Yellow Book of Lecan*, held in Trinity College, Dublin, and in other manuscripts.]

Deirdre

*or The Exile of the Sons of Uisliu
and the Death of Deirdre*

ℰ

Feidhlimidh mac Daill was entertaining Conchobhor, king of Ulster, and his men at his house. They were all drunk. Feidhlimidh, who was the king's storyteller, was urging his wife to make sure that no-one's cup remained unfilled. She rushed about, and was on her feet all night, even though she was heavily pregnant and her time nearly upon her. She ran back and forth from the fire, handing round cuts of meat and replenishing drinks as the noise of drunken revelry increased. She stayed up, looking after them, until they had all fallen into their beds, dead drunk. When they were all asleep, she passed through the quiet house and as she did the child in her womb gave such a shriek that the men got up from where they lay with each other, and stumbled back into the hall, and there they stood, staring at each other, bleary-eyed. Then Sencha, Conchobhor's chief adviser, spoke:

"Everyone, be still. Feidhlimidh, bring the woman here so that we can find out what made this scream." And so Feidhlimidh went to her and said:

"What is this clamour in your womb? Do you know you have hurt everyone's ears. I'm scared of what you are carrying inside you." He was roaring at her in rage.

She ran over to Cathbhadh, who was a druid and prophet and seer. She said to him: "Cathbhadh, you have a gentle face; you are kind and dignified. You understand patience, toil, and study. What am I to say to a husband who is confused and overwrought by this strange event? I have a certain amount of magic, that I can use for others, but like many another such I am at a loss when it comes to my own case. What am I carrying? What has screamed inside me?"

"A child with yellow hair cried out from your womb", said Cathbhadh. Already her head is covered in thick, matted curls. Her eyes are a cold clear blue. And her cheeks have the purple tinge of the foxglove hidden in their whiteness. Her teeth are like snow and her lips bright crimson. She is a woman who will cause slaughter and murder all over Ulster and beyond. Champions will fight over her; kings will ask other kings if they have seen her; queens will envy her slim and flawless body."

Then Cathbhadh put his hand on the woman's swollen stomach, and the child inside kicked so hard he felt its tiny foot.

"All I'm saying", he went on, "is true. The child you are carrying is a girl. Her name will be Deirdre, and she will bring sorrow and misfortune with her."

And there, in front of them all, the woman began to give birth and the baby was born. As she was emerging into the world the druid Cathbhadh made this prophesy:

"Deirdre, girl, you will bring sorrow to many. Slaughter will follow your actions and shadow all you do. You will bring suffering to Ulster. Your beauty will arouse jealousy and possessiveness. You will cause a whole family of brothers to be exiled. And a great wrong will be done at Emhain Macha, which will originate with you, because of your determination to do what you want. You will commit the vilest of acts against the majesty of the king of Ulster himself. You are misfortune itself to all who see you now."

The men of Ulster were all still crowded around the woman holding the bloody child in her arms. They were frightened when they heard Cathbhadh's solemn words. First one, then another, then all together shouted:

"Kill her. Kill her. Kill her."

But Conchobhor himself, shouting above the noise and roaring, said: "No".

When the shouting subsided he went on, speaking more quietly, but in an authoritative and firm even tone:

"Tomorrow I will take her from here. I will foster her in a quiet place. I will outline the most careful instructions for her nurse and foster-father and she will be brought up a quiet, careful, steady, and judicious woman. And then when she arrives at a marriageable age I'll take her as my own wife, so that I will personally counteract any trace of evil she may still retain even after such a careful education and fosterage."

No-one, not even Cathbhadh the druid, had the nerve to speak out against the king when he had so clearly determined on this course of action, although they all had the deepest misgivings.

The king returned to Emhain Macha. He carried the baby in his arms as he was driven in a chariot, and he looked down at her startling blue eyes, open to the sky, and at her red lips. He called to his chamber at the palace a wise woman, Lebhorcham, and put her in charge of the girl's upbringing. Lebhorcham was respected for her knowledge and for her skill as a healer, but she was also feared because of her magical powers. No-one dared cross her for fear of being cursed by her. Conchobhor assigned to her an isolated house and enclosure in the woods some way from Emhain Macha. Conchobhor also provided Deirdre with foster-parents, but apart from these three no-one else was allowed to go into the hidden fort in the forest. There, as the years went by, Deirdre grew up to be the loveliest woman in Ireland.

One day, many years later, Deirdre's foster-father was out in front of the fort, skinning a calf. It was winter, and a heavy snow had fallen. A raven flew down and began to drink the calf's blood, startling and red on the white snow. Deirdre was looking out at this with Lebhorcham, and she said:

"Any man with those three colours would have my love: hair like the raven, skin with the whiteness of snow, and crimson red in his cheek."

"There is", said her nurse, "a man like the one you describe. He its called Naoise, the son of Uisliu, and he is a great warrior of Ulster. I am sorry to tell you this, because misfortune is surely gathering for you, but maybe you will be lucky, and maybe you will live in peace and honour."

"Whatever about that", said Deirdre, "I'll not rest till I lay eyes on him."

One day not long afterwards Naoise was out on the earthen

rampart surrounding Emhain Macha, singing to himself in his sweet tenor voice. All the sons of Uisliu had extraordinarily beautiful voices which made their listeners serene and peaceful and happy. At times he would stop singing, and relax, before practising the martial blocking techniques for which he and his brothers were equally famous.

Something told Deirdre that Naoise was out on this rampart,

alone. She ran swiftly through the forest, not knowing where she was going, until she broke through the trees and came to the steep green bank. She glimpsed Naoise on top of the rampart and was shocked at his beauty. But she steadied herself, and walked slowly into the opening between the forest and the wall where he could see her. He looked down at the girl:

"There's a fine heifer down there in front of me", he said.

"If bulls", she said, "aren't big enough then heifers must be."

Hearing this reply, and looking at her, he realized in terror who this was: Deirdre, the fateful girl, reserved for Conchobhor.

"You are going to have the biggest bull of the whole of Ulster, the king himself", said he.

"I'm prepared to choose for myself. And between you and him I'd pick a fine young virile bull like you any day".

"This cannot be", he said. "Have you not heard of Cathbhadh's prophecy, made at your birth?"

"Are you trying to get rid of me?" she asked, standing straight in front of him. "Come down and face me."

This Naoise did. Again she asked him if he was trying to get rid of her.

"Exactly so", he replied. "Everyone knows the disaster you are meant to bring, and understands that the king thinks he can check it with his own power."

With that she leapt at him and caught him by the ears, pulling at them and laughing.

"By these ears you will be a disgrace to all men if you don't take me out of here with you. Have you no courage?"

"Go away from me", he said, trying to push her away, and frightened.

"You have no choice", she said. "You're now compelled by your honour and my will. That is that."

Naoise, knowing there was no escape, sat down on the

ground and began to sing, sorrowfully. She pitied him even as she desired him.

"Leave me", he said, "for a while. I'll go to you and bring you away with me, but first I must tell my brothers, Ardán and Ainnle."

She went back through the woods, amazed at what she had done. Naoise went into Emhain Macha and told his brothers that he was going to abduct Deirdre at her own command.

"What are you thinking of?" said Ardán.

"What is the matter with you?" said Ainnle. "Nothing but sorrow and bad luck can come of this."

"If you do this we can't stay here in Ulster", said Ardán. "You're condemning all of us to exile."

"I know", said Naoise. "There is nothing I can do."

"Shame and dishonour and unrest will follow us for the rest of our lives", said Ainnle.

"We'll have to go tonight", said Ardán, "before this news breaks. Let us take a hundred and fifty warriors and go as soon as we can."

And that was what they did. They rode into the forest and Deirdre ran out to meet them, and then they were gone, travelling southwest to Assaroe, and then onwards over the Shannon into the wild places of Munster, turning northwards again towards Howth. All the time they had to keep moving, spending only one night at each camping place, because Conchobhor's men followed them.

Meanwhile the king sent emissaries to all the kings of Ireland, telling them what the sons of Uisliu had done to him, and asking them to waylay them or kill them. So that even when some local king would offer them protection they were never sure if they could trust him, and all the time they kept on the move.

Eventually, exhausted from travelling and harassed by the fear of real or imagined treachery, they went over to Scotland, where they lived for a while in the Highlands, feeding on the wild deer and other game. After some time they gained the protection of a king there in exchange for which they offered their skills as soldiers and raiders. They lived inside the royal enclosure but they insisted their dwellings be constructed in such a way as to prevent any one visiting the brothers from seeing Deirdre. Naoise

knew that if any other man saw her killing and slaughter would certainly follow.

However, early one morning, a servant looked in through a window where a curtain had been left partly undrawn, and saw her sleeping naked in Naoise's arms. Wild with excitement and lust he ran to the king, and woke him up.

"What do you think you're doing?" roared the Scottish king.

"I've never", panted the servant, "seen till this day a woman worthy of you. But the woman lying with Naoise is fit to be the queen of the western world. Go now and kill him while he's sleeping and have her immediately, while her dead husband lies beside her."

"No", said the king. "But you can go, every day, in secret, and ask her if she will be my woman."

This the servant did and every day Deirdre refused him. The king now began sending the sons of Uisliu into the most dangerous situations in battle, hoping that they would be killed, but they were such ferocious and skilled fighters that they survived all his tricks and ploys. Eventually, the king decided to gather a huge force and attack their houses within his enclosure. The servant told Deirdre of the king's plan, as a last attempt to get her to yield, but she would not, and told the three men. That night they fled under cover of darkness and went to Islay off the coast of Scotland.

News came to Ulster of their plight and the attempt against

them by the Scots. Some of his men decided to speak to Conchobhor about them. They sat in conclave, and after much argument, one said to the king:

"Take pity on the sons of Uisliu", he said. "They are in enemy territory, and will continue to be attacked, and all of this through the wilfulness and evil of one bad woman. You must be kingly and show leniency. Forgive them. Send for them and let them come home before they are killed by the Scots."

Conchobhor thought, then said:

"Let them come back to Ulster. As a token of our goodwill we will send to them, as pledges of our sincerity, Fergus, Dubhthach and Cormac."

Fergus was an old and respected warrior, who had given up the kingship in favour of Conchobhor; Dubhthach was one of the most trusted of all the king's advisers; and Cormac was Conchobhor's own son.

So they went and carried the king's message to the sons of Uisliu on Islay, explaining they were sent as an earnest of the king's sincerity, not just as emissaries. The sons of Uisliu were overcome with joy and relief when they heard the offer and gladly accepted. They and Deirdre sailed from Islay, Fergus and the others with them. However, as soon as they reached the Antrim coast, the first of Conchobhor's traps lay waiting for them. He had arranged that the local king offer Fergus an invitation to an ale-feast. Because of an old oath he had sworn, vowing never to

mad battle rage and the slaughter went on all day and all night. Dubhthach, one by one, dragged the women of Emhain Macha out from their hiding places, and killed them. Fergus, eventually, when those who were not dead had fled the enclosure, set fire to the whole place and burnt it to the ground. Dubhthach and Cormac then left Ulster, vowing to remain its enemies forever,

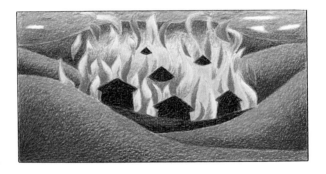

and went to join with Medhbh, queen of Connacht, and Ailill, her husband. Three thousand men of Ulster went with them to join Medhbh's army.

Deirdre lived with Conchobhor for a year, and during that time she did not smile, she barely ate, hardly ever slept, and always sat with her face in her hands over her knees. Sometimes Conchobhor would try to cheer her by having musicians play to her, but all it did was to remind her of Naoise, and then she would sing, in a voice full of sorrow:

> While I washed you, Naoise,
> before the fire, I would drink
> the hazel mead you made
> and watch the meat darken on the spit.

> You would prepare the stones
> for cooking in the forest, and the food
> was sweet as if baked in honey
> with herbs of lavender and sorrel.

> I long for the deep melody
> of Naoise's voice that held
> the shock of the sea-wave,
> the sorrow of the dark wood.

> I hardly sleep anymore;
> I do not colour my fingernails
> with red paint; there's no joy
> in my life now Naoise's gone.

Sometimes Conchobhor would try to talk her our of her sadness, and she would reply:

"You love me but it is as nothing to me now that a small

mound of black stones covers that white body. My sorrow is stronger than the sea."

One day Conchobhor asked her who she hated most of all in the world:

"You", she replied, "and Eoghan mac Durthacht."

"Then", he said, "you've spent a year with me. You can now spend a year with him."

And so he brought her to Eoghan. The following day all three went to the fair at Emhain Macha. Eoghan was handling the traces of the chariot, she was behind him, and Conchobhor stood behind her. She had sworn to herself that she would never look on these two men together. Conchobhor noticed her agitation.

"Well", he said, "the way you look between Eoghan and myself is like a sheep between two rams."

The chariot was coming up to a big boulder with a large outcrop on it. She leaned out and smashed her head against it, shattering the skull into a mass of fragments, and died instantly.

[This retelling is based on the version of the tale preserved in the *Book of Leinster* and edited by Vernam Hull as *Longes mac nUislenn* (1949).]

Glossary and
Pronounciation Guide

❦

This guide contains explanations of some of the more important Irish names in these stories as well as an approximate indication as to how these names are pronounced. Throughout the translated text names are given in modern spelling, i.e. Sliabh is spelt so, not Sliab, the Old and Middle Irish orthography.

Aebh: pr. Aev.

Aodh: pr. Ae.

Bodhbh Dearg: pr. Bov Darg.

Cathbhadh: druid to king Conchobhor, pr. Cothvad.

Conchobhor: king of the men of Ulster, the Ulaid; pr. Crohoore.

Crunnchu mac Agnomhain: pr. Crunn-hoo mock Ag-no-van.

Daghda: pr. Die-da.

Dáire Doidgheal: Daire of the White Hand, pr. Daw-ir-e Dough-id-yal.

Deoch: pr. Dioc.

Dubh Ruis: pr. Duv Rish.

Emhain Macha: Navan Fort in Co. Armagh; pr. Owin Maha.

Eoghan mac Durthacht: pr. Owen mock Dur-hoct.

Feidhlimidh mac Daill: pr. File-im-ee mock Dyle.

Feidhlim: pr. Faylim.

Fiachra: Fee-ah-ra.

Lairgnéan: pr. Largnayon.

Lebhorcham: pr. Lev-ur-ham.

Medhbh: queen of Connacht; pr. Maeve.

Mochaemóg: literally "the Youth"; pr. Mohaveoge.

Naoise: pr. Nee-shi.

Noínden Ulad: translated as "the Debility of the Men of Ulster" , though literally "the Novena of the Men of Ulster", from the nine periods of time - five days, four nights - during which they suffered the debility drawn down upon them by Macha's curse.

Ochón ó : alas, alas; pr. uchone, oh.

ogham: a Celtic alphabet based upon marks made along a line. Often used on grave slabs; pr. oh-am.

Sencha mac Ailill: pr. Shen-ha mock Alill.

Sliabh Mis: mountain near Tralee, Co. Kerry; pr. Sleeov Mish.

Tuatha Dé Danann: predecessors to the Celts (or Gaels) as settlers of Ireland who, after their defeat, retired to the raths or fairy-mounds and became the fairies. Literally: people of the goddess Danu; pr. Too-a-ha day don-ann.